THE BATTLE OF
TRAFALGAR

MACMILLAN · BATTLE BOOKS

THE MACMILLAN BATTLE BOOKS ARE PREPARED UNDER
THE GENERAL EDITORSHIP OF EDWARD R. SAMMIS

THE BATTLE OF
TRAFALGAR

Lord Nelson Sweeps the Sea

★

By ALAN VILLIERS

THE MACMILLAN COMPANY, NEW YORK
COLLIER–MACMILLAN LIMITED, LONDON

The Macmillan Company, New York
Collier-Macmillan Canada, Ltd., Toronto, Ontario
Library of Congress catalog card number: 65-15169

Picture credits: L. Dorado, 23, 45, 68, 78; Library of Congress, 26, 50–51; Montagu Motor Museum, Beaulieu, England, 36, 38, 39, 89; Musée de la Marine, Paris, 54, 55; National Maritime Museum, Greenwich, England, title page, 9, 10, 13, 15, 16–17, 19, 22, 24, 31, 36, 41, 49, 53, 63, 65 (Greenwich Hospital Collection), 66–67, 74–75, 79 (Greenwich Hospital Collection), 82–83, 85, 87; United Press International, 42, 90. Picture editing by Gabriele Wunderlich.

Maps by Hamilton Greene
Designed by Alan Benjamin
Printed in the United States of America
First Printing

940.2
V752b

CONTENTS

★

CHAPTER ONE

"WITH JOYFUL ACCLAMATION"

"The joyful acclamations of the watch on deck announced that we were near the enemy, who were in line under easy sail a few miles to leeward. . . ."

"As the day dawned the horizon appeared covered with ships. . . ."

"I was awakened by the cheers of the crew as they rushed up the hatchways to get a glimpse of the hostile fleet. Their delight exceeded anything I ever witnessed. . . ."

So wrote three English midshipmen before the Battle of Trafalgar. What made them so happy? Before nightfall, hundreds of them would be dead.

In the dawn of that Monday morning in October, 1805, they saw the combined fleets of Napoleonic France and her temporary ally Spain, under sail, making from their Spanish base port of Cádiz, a long line of stately great ships with their high hulls burnished and their graceful sails golden in the sun. They were some 12 miles from Cape Trafalgar when first sighted, not far from the Strait of Gibraltar, and they were sailing toward the Mediterranean, where Napoleon had ordered them to go.

What the seamen cheered was the prospect of battle: a slogging, all-out, bloody fight in their beautiful ships, under a small, quiet seaman—one-armed, one-eyed—who by God's grace and his country's good fortune was the greatest admiral in the world. Lord Nelson! His very name was terror to his enemies, inspiration to his friends and followers. On that day, he had one purpose: the wiping of the Franco-Spanish fleet from the face of the sea.

The destruction of that fleet would cripple the efforts of the French dictator Napoleon Bonaparte—called Napoleon— to dominate the world. Not just its defeat, but its destruction was essential.

For years, Napoleon, with his brilliant tactics, had menaced Europe and the world. Bursting out of a France vitalized by successful revolution, splendid French armies fighting under his genius had overrun all Europe, threatened the peace of the world. One country only—England—they had never defeated, nor dared to invade. The English Channel made the island invulnerable to the most able general so long as he lacked command of the sea. For this, he needed a great fleet, an armada of fighting men.

It was Napoleon's last great fleet that those English seamen saw that "beautiful, misty, sun-shiny morning." Smash that and the immediate result would be that England—their home —could not be invaded: the long-term outcome must be Napoleon's ruin.

The Long Chase

The British cheered and cheered! For their great difficulty had been to catch that fleet at sea, to make its huge ships fight where they could not run for the shelter of base ports, to lie in safety while their enemies prowled outside—endlessly, apparently fruitlessly.

This, many of those English ships had been doing for eighty-four weeks—eighty-four weeks on end. No leave, no respite, no change except of location—sometimes (most often) in the Mediterranean, sometimes in the stormy Bay of Biscay and off the shores of France, once right across the North Atlantic when a wily French admiral named Villeneuve slipped out of base, dashed away to the West Indies and back again, the English sea dogs after him.

They did not catch him that time. Villeneuve sailed back to Europe and landlocked his ships in their battery-protected bases.

Always outside, the English waited, watching, sometimes with a few frigates—their lighter ships, swift but poorly armed, watchdogs but not fighting ships-of-the-line—while the big ships ranged farther out, within call. Day after day, week after week, month after month, year after year. . . . It seemed that it would never end.

Once, seven years earlier, Admiral Nelson *had* caught a French fleet, anchored in a port where he could sail in and attack them, although to do so meant accepting dangerous odds. The French were anchored close inshore, with batteries protecting them, near the port of Alexandria, on the Mediterranean coast of Egypt. Inside the French fleet was shoal water, where ships would go aground.

The French admiral thought that such an anchorage was impregnable. He had landed some of his men and ships' guns.

Nelson noticed that the French ships were swinging freely at their anchors, not moored, as seamen describe the safer method of securing ships with big anchors at both ends to prevent them from drifting about.

Nelson prepares to engage Villeneuve's fleet off Trafalgar.

The climax of the Battle of the Nile at Abukir, August 1, 1798

If the French ships had water enough to swing in, there was water enough for the English ships to sail in, too, inside that anchored line of too-confident ships.

So Nelson, with his smaller English fleet, sailed by night right into the congested, shoal-filled bay, beside the great ships of France. Cannon roared, flames belched, smoke of battle rose high to the starlit heavens, reddened by the glow of exploding ships—all French. . . . Before morning, the fighting power of that fleet was destroyed. Seamen called this the Battle of the Nile.

But the force destroyed was only part of French sea power. Though its loss wrecked Napoleon's plans to take Egypt and dominate the Indian Ocean—seize India and its rich trade, all Indonesia, and the new continent of Australia—the blow was not mortal.

Now, years later, upon this bright October morning, that forest of great ships sailing by Cape Trafalgar eastward for the Mediterranean was the last effective sea strength of France, with a squadron of splendid Spanish ships in company.

Destroy them! But how?

The land was near, the wind light, the Franco-Spanish fleet in obvious superiority of ships and fire power. But at last Nelson had caught them with sea room to fight in, at last he had time to attack before they could get back to base. No wonder the English cheered.

To get those Napoleonic warships where he wanted them, Nelson had hidden his big ships, kept them far at sea, accepted the enemy's superior numbers and the apparently heavy odds against him.

In the dawn light, the Franco-Spanish fleet, silhouetted against the rising sun, added up to 33 ships, strung out in a long line. Among them were several mighty vessels, including the *Santissima Trinidad*, the only four-decker, the largest and —with 138 guns—most heavily armed ship in the world.

Against these splendid ships, the English had 27, the largest of them armed with 100 guns apiece. On this relatively small force, Lord Nelson was staking his future—and the fate of the world's two most potent navies.

Lord Nelson

Who was this Lord Nelson, this scourge of the sea? A grim-faced, stern-jawed sea dog, resolute and domineering? Or a reckless, swashbuckling daredevil? A bulwark of the quarter-deck, fire in his nostrils, salt water for blood, the roar of the storm in his mighty voice, and icy reserve in his human relations?

Far from all these things, the famous admiral, with his slight figure, soft face, boyish and sensitive, looked more like a poet than a fighting seaman. A physical weakling as a child and never strong afterward, he would have passed no medical-board examination for sea service if such had then been required.

Horatio Nelson was the sixth of eleven children in the family of an English parson, Edmund Nelson, the rector of a place called Burnham Thorpe in the county of Norfolk, within sight of the cold North Sea. Here Nelson was born on September 29, 1758. The driving sails of ships in storms were in distant sight from his window, and the biting east winds blowing in from sea nearly killed him as a small child. But ships became his passion—any ships; above all, fighting ships.

Few boys seemed less fitted to follow such a hard and boisterous life.

"Why should poor Horatio be sent to rough it at sea?" his naval-captain uncle had asked when requested to find a place for him. Why, indeed? At the age of twelve, it was the little boy's wish. He knew what he wanted.

So his uncle, Captain Maurice Suckling, got the lad on the ship he commanded, and off to sea he went. The year was 1770, the occasion a war scare with Spain over the Falkland Islands.

The scare passed, for the moment. The uncle sent the small boy to serve for a year in a merchant brig—a tough little two-master—to learn the seaman's business. A crowded warship was a poor place for a twelve-year-old midshipman. His experiences on the brig during a voyage to the West Indies taught young Nelson many things—among them, to understand the working seaman.

Vice-Admiral Horatio Nelson (portrait by Hoppner)

A voyage to the Arctic, a long voyage in Indian seas and to the Persian Gulf, the West Indies again—this time in a ship of war—and service during the American Revolution gave the boy experience. "Dreadfully seasick"—his own words—near dead of fevers in both the East Indies and the West, he prospered in his tough profession nonetheless.

Promotion came fast. Nelson was a post captain before he was twenty-one—the highest rank reached by promotion; elevation to admiral (Nelson became a rear admiral in 1797, a vice-admiral in 1801) was by seniority among the captains and was a long wait, sometimes shortened by wars.

"The merest boy of a captain I ever beheld," remarked a future British king—Prince William Henry—who met him at this time, adding after some conversation with Nelson that he was "no common being."

He was born in a time of action, in a heroic age of British naval victories and achievement. He inherited a splendid fighting fleet from a long line of illustrious fighting admirals. Yet he was racked by pain from badly healed and poorly treated wounds, hypersensitive, emotional, and sometimes vain. He could be boastful too.

"I have all the diseases there are, but not enough in my body for them to fasten on," he wrote. Yet he seemed to be made of steel. Once, with his right elbow shattered (later, his arm had to be removed) in a violent action ashore, and white with loss of blood, he insisted on climbing unaided up the high side of his ship on his return. He was the captain: no one could stop him.

"I have my legs left, and one arm," he said. But it took him desperate months to recover from that wound. A few years before, he had lost an eye. Yet the tremendous flood of real humanity that made him outstanding as a man never left him.

A long view of the two fleets
(painting by Pocock)

there upon the inshore waters of the Atlantic Ocean, rolling so quietly and with—for the moment—such peaceful and perfect beauty, he saw the enemy fleet begin to make a turn. Each ship, in response to signals, went through the evolution which caused her to turn back toward the port of Cádiz, forming a great long line that sagged a little in the middle. Nelson's determination was that most of them would never make Cádiz. None at all, if he could help it.

With a slow hoist of flag signals, the 27 English ships changed course, slowly and with grace, to come up with the French and Spanish.

The big ships pitched and rolled gently in the slight sea; with the motion, wind-filled sails slatted and jerked at their tacks and sheets; the complicated fabric of towering riggings creaked and the wooden hulls groaned. The wind sang softly in all the high riggings—too softly for such massive, heavy-built sailing ships as these. There was not breeze enough to let them sail faster than a man could walk.

No matter. More wind will come. The stage is set.

Nelson is ready. Forming his fleet in two lines, he leads the first toward the leading ships of the enemy. His friend and second-in-command Vice-Admiral Collingwood leads the second. Collingwood and all the captains review exactly what they have to do, for Nelson has written it all out in a memorandum days before.

It might look, for the moment, as though he is heading for the leading French and Spanish ships in more or less orthodox formation. This is to fool them. In fact, he is determined to break through their line in two formations, to sail across them, right in among them, cut the greater part off, and destroy them!

Before the cutoff leaders can turn and sail back to support

Lord Nelson discusses the British battle plan with his officers.

their struggling consorts, it will be too late. It takes time for such ships to turn and sail back the way they have come.

When they get there, they will be a minority too. Nelson's tactics, though dangerous, mean that his smaller fleet will first assail and destroy the enemy's cutoff center and rear. By cutting into them, *once his ships have fought their way through*, he can convert their superiority in numbers to inferiority and can deal with them piecemeal. When the leading ships sail back into the action—if they can make it—they can be dealt with in their turn. It's all spelled out in the little admiral's memorandum.

And yet, orders thought out before a battle cannot be perfect.

"Something must be left to chance," Nelson has written, in assigning full control of his own column to Collingwood. ". . . No captain can do very wrong if he places his ship alongside that of an enemy."

Once having done that, there was no doubt of the result.

★

CHAPTER TWO

BEAT TO QUARTERS!

BEAT TO QUARTERS! Suddenly the drums roll. Pipes shrill. Bare feet patter on scrubbed steps of companionways. Hatches swing open. Lids of gun ports lift slowly outward and upward. Wicked black muzzles of heavy guns, trundled forward on their wooden-wheeled carriages, peer brutishly at the sea. Colors flutter aloft in the morning wind.

A line of boys and "waisters"—the least experienced seamen—pass up sacks of sand from the hold. The sand is sprinkled copiously on the gun decks and wetted with sea water, for it must assure surviving gunners a foothold when the blood runs.

The decks well wetted against fire and sanded against blood, up come the powder bags, placed carefully by each gun to be handy but not too close to be easily set on fire. The carpenters and their gangs clear the decks; they pull down surplus bulkheads, stow furniture below, throw overboard all that is not easily stowed; the one-legged cook douses his galley flame—all this to minimize risk of fire, reduce the combustibles in these so burnable wooden ships.

Aloft, the best sailors run like monkeys to rig preventer

gear, so that the heavy yards will not come tumbling down when rigging is shot away. A lithe midshipman in his uniform of blue and gold and white races to the mastheads to lash the national colors there. If the flag is shot away, another must be shown! For the flagless ship may be considered as out of the fight, surrendered.

Deep in the ship's dark innards, the surgeon prepares his grim "clinic." The light of a few lanterns shines weakly on his operating table, a board covered with a doubled sheet of scrubbed sailcloth. The surgeon and his assistants, sleeves rolled up, lay out knives, scalpels, saws, sponges, and stout lint to check hemorrhages, line up clean strips of thick leather to thrust into patients' mouths during the screaming pain of amputations. They open a keg of rum and rig tubs into which to fling cut-off arms and legs.

No one will walk in here. Whoever can walk can fight. The seamen and their officers are *tough*, of a fiber now unknown, boasting of their blood of Stockholm tar, hair of hempen yarn, hearts of oak, beards of marlinespikes. Inured to hardships in a harsh world where weaklings die young and unmourned, they are ready to take it as it comes.

Black-silk handkerchiefs tied around their heads and ears to deaden the terrible din, shirt sleeves tucked up, crowbars and handspikes of their gun's gear in their strong hands, naked cutlasses at their belts, they look like happy devils. Powder boys, their preparations done, sit upon their boxes full of powder, waiting.

Butterflies may flutter in a few boyish stomachs as the long morning drags by. Youngest powder monkey aboard the *Victory* is ten-year-old Johnny Doag, rated "Boy, First Class." Four others are barely twelve.

Among the crew of more than six hundred are twenty-two

A British seaman entertains shipmates with a yarn belowdecks.

Americans, as well as Portuguese, some West Indians, an African, and several Frenchmen.

Captains of the 100 guns buckle on their priming boxes. Officers stand with drawn swords by their divisions, an alert eye on everything.

In the French and Spanish ships, the scene and the activity are much the same. The captains, each attended by his first lieutenant and suite, make the rounds of their gun decks. Powdered wigs, colorful uniforms, glittering swords distinguish them as the drums and fifes march before them. All here is also in readiness—the wet sand, the powder, and the shot, the ghastly preparations for surgery. Extra battle ensigns fly from high aloft. Each Spanish ship has hoisted a large wooden cross above the quarter-deck, where all may see it.

The great figurehead of the enormous *Santissima Trinidad* —colossal white figures representing the Holy Trinity— overlooks the next ship in line-ahead. Her gloriously gilded and ornamented stern rolls slowly beneath the headsails of the next astern. Her 138 guns poke their black muzzles—

ready to belch red flames and red-hot cannon balls—from the crimson-and-white sides of the magnificent ship. Her crew of more than a thousand men and boys stand ready at their quarters, while a full band on deck blares martial music.

One preparation goes on aboard the French and Spanish ships which is neglected in the English. Marines in full uniform and all accouterments, dragging their long muskets with them, climb slowly up their rigging to the "tops"—open platforms at the lower mastheads, as large as small classrooms, where normally the "topmen" stand by to tend the rigging. These "tops," with their bird's-eye view of the deck below, are ideal spots for sharpshooters. Ammunition is passed up, muskets loaded. Grenades are passed up too.

The Santissima Trinidad *boasted 138 guns and a crew of 1,048.*

English custom was that better use could be made of men on the gun decks. Motion could be excessive up a sailing ship's mast. Aim was difficult, especially with the inefficient muskets of those days. There was some risk of fire with those old weapons. And men up at the mastheads might never get a useful shot in at all.

"*Vive l'empereur! Vive le commandant!*" shout the gunners and the seamen, the powder monkeys and the ships' boys sailing to their deaths.

The ships roll onward with stately grace, slowly, inexorably, still in the same formation—but imperfectly kept with the wind so light. Ships' sailing qualities differ. Station-keeping in line-ahead is difficult.

Leading the English windward line is H.M.S. *Victory*,

Lord Nelson's warship, the Victory, *rigged and ready for battle*

a 100-gunner, more than 2,000 tons, 40 years old. Colling-wood leads the leeward column in another 100-gunner, the *Royal Sovereign.*

Collingwood changes into a fresh uniform, pulls off his heavy sea boots, shifts into clean silk stockings and shoes.

"They are so much more manageable for the surgeon," he says with a smile to his flag lieutenant, and goes back on the quarter-deck.

All the morning, the fleets sail on, for the wind remains light.

By his unorthodox tactics, Lord Nelson risks a lot. His ships must sail slowly, straight toward a massive and seemingly impregnable line of the most powerful warships in the world, which outnumber him in ships, men, and guns. Because all such ships could fire their guns only directly to either side, an approaching vessel exposed herself to the full weight of her opponents' broadsides, while she could reply only with a few bow guns.

This is not the usual manner of line-of-battle fights, which was for opposing fleets to sail in more or less parallel line-ahead and slug it out broadside to broadside.

Both the *Victory* and the *Royal Sovereign* take a big chance on being blown clean out of the water as soon as they come within range. Ship after ship following behind them may easily share the same fate, one by one, in fatal turn—if they ever get that far.

Even more easily, they may be dismasted, their high masts and heavy yards and all the pattern of their sails brought to nothing, smashed about their ears. Helpless hulks upon the water then, unable to maneuver or even to move, how could they fight? What could they do but lie upon the sea, stopped and helpless?

LEFT: *Vice-Admiral Cuthbert Collingwood, leader of the leeward line.* RIGHT: *Sir Thomas Masterman Hardy, the* Victory's *captain*

French and Spanish gunners loaded their guns with double-shot—two cannon balls chained loosely together—to roar through rigging, smash spars and sails, and tear down masts. Each of the approaching ships could be—*should* be—dismasted in turn. Broadside guns could be levered a little this way and that to fire at an angle, and their breeches could be lowered and muzzles raised to fire high. It was difficult to take aim from a rolling deck by peering along the gun. Good judgment had to estimate the time lag between the touch of fire to the small opening above the powder and the actual explosion that expelled the cannon ball. The ship might roll the muzzle up, sending the ball uselessly too high, or down, firing the shot into the sea. It took time and well-drilled, cool-headed crews to reload and aim properly.

Good gunnery was vital. The more experienced British were then far better gunners, man for man, than the Spanish and French.

Within Range

No one knows all this better than the little admiral.

High on the *Victory*'s quarter-deck, he walks unconcernedly, up and down with the ship's captain, Thomas Masterman Hardy. Dressed in his vice-admiral's uniform, the stars of his four decorations embroidered on the frock coat for all to see, he chats with Captain Hardy. In bringing the Franco-Spanish fleet to action, his real work is done. His second-in-command and all his captains know what they have to do, which is to cut the enemy off from base, sail through their line regardless, attack any and every ship they can get at once they are through, destroy, annihilate—every ship for itself and utter confusion for the enemy.

Having put them advantageously in position, an admiral with confidence in them and sure of their confidence in him could do no more.

Until now, Nelson has led his column toward the enemy van on a converging course, in order that Villeneuve might not be certain of his intentions. Now, by midmorning, the fleets are closer, the Franco-Spanish line sagging in its center toward the land, in a crescent formation.

Alter course! Around swings the *Victory*, ponderous but glorious, with a singing of tackles, a swishing of sails, a shouted response to the new steering orders at the wheel. Around come her consorts each in turn, headed now to smash into the enemy line a ship or two ahead of its center, where their commanding admiral should be.

The enemy van lumbers on, drawing farther away.

Shortly after noon, the *Victory* is at last within range. She sails on silently, rolling a little, pitching heavily, the wind behind her. The amazing silence of the silent sailing ships surrounds her, as if the wind and sea are awed by the threat of the impending battle, eager to hold the beautiful pageantry of the glorious sailing ships until the last possible moment, for the sea will never behold their like in such battle again.

The thundering flash of crimson flame suddenly annihilates all peace.

Bang! Bang! Crash!

Flames lick along the black gun mouths on the *Santissima Trinidad*'s side, along the guns of the French admiral's *Bucentaure* and half a dozen other French and Spanish ships. Smoke belches, seconds after the flames, and billows over the sea. The Franco-Spanish line stands like the solid wall of a fortified city, massive, apparently indestructible.

Again the guns roar, again and again. Whenever the smoke clears, there the great, frightening line of the ponderous ships stands solid on the sea.

Still the *Victory*, the *Royàl Sovereign*, and their lines of consorts sail on, apparently unscathed, impervious to the heavy gunfire—but not quite. As yet, they cannot fire in return.

Cannon balls strike the *Victory*, bounce off her 3-foot-thick wooden sides, smash over her quarter-deck, break through the mizzen-topmast. One strikes the quarter-deck very near the admiral, tears his secretary almost in half, rips up splinters that fly everywhere, knocks the steering wheel to pieces and the silver buckles from one of Hardy's shoes.

"Warm work, Hardy," says the little admiral. "Too hot to last long."

They go on walking.

Vice-Admiral Pierre
Silvestre de Villeneuve

Still the English cannot reply. It's the risk that Nelson has accepted. He glances aloft. Apart from the mizzen—the least important mast—the *Victory's* rigging is intact. The enemy fire is erratic, as he knew it would be. Too long in port.

The *Victory* sails on.

Now, out of the smoke above them towers the *Santissima Trinidad*. Jammed almost into her, another great ship follows, then another and another, like a troop of outsize circus elephants trunk to tail. Instead of breaking through between them the *Victory* must sail *at* one.

"Where shall I head for?" shouts Hardy above the din.

"My good Hardy, it does not signify—take your choice!"

But a way opens. A slight freshening of the wind, a slight increase in the swell and the English flagship, skillfully handled, is thrusting her bowsprit between the French ships *Bucentaure* and *Redoutable,* her jib boom lost in smoke, her

apple-cheeked bows easing a path for her, her gilded figurehead fierce and unmoved at the high cutwater, shining in the
smoky sunshine like the head of a god. With a violent crunch-
ing together of powerful ships, a banging, quivering, and
crashing as the swell shakes them, the crash of torn woodwork
and splintered spars, the thunder of ripped and shot-torn sails,
three ships lock together, for the moment, in a melee of
cannon blast and smoke and flame.

Above it all, in a lull of the wild firing, comes another
sound—the swelling roar of English cheering.

At last, at long and dreadful last, bravely awaited, the fight
is on!

Already Collingwood has broken through, nearer the rear.
Before the gunsmoke envelopes that part of the sea, Nelson
sees that they have made it. The leading second-line ships
are giving battle, their masts still intact, everything under
control, going according to plan.

And now it is the little admiral's turn.

As she bursts through the line, the *Victory*'s cold guns
warm up at last. They pour broadside after broadside through
the stern of the French *Bucentaure* on the one hand and into
the length of the *Redoutable* on the other. Double- and
treble-shotted cannon balls cause carnage on both sides.

Crashing through the glass windows of the unprotected
stern, through the gilt work, the carvings, and the ginger-
bread, the murderous cannon balls, held back so long, now
sweep like a scythe swinging in soft corn through the lengths
of the gun decks of the *Bucentaure*, mowing down men,
knocking guns from their mountings, destroying, pulverizing,
doing damage irreparably.

Into the *Redoutable* she pours grapeshot at point-blank
range with a broadside so heavy that the whole ship reels.

Her guns blazing, the Victory *smashes through the French line.*

Swinging through the gap of her own making, her yards passing directly over the now mangled quarter-deck of one ship and the broken bows of the other, the *Victory* falls alongside the *Redoutable* in a flaming, terrible embrace. Gunners race to reload.

All around, as other English ships come up to the line and break through or fall alongside enemies standing in their way, the great battle becomes what Nelson intended—a series of ferocious, bloody ship-to-ship close-quarter fights in which the best men and the best-fighting ships must win.

"No captain can do very wrong if he places his ship alongside that of an enemy."

So Nelson had said. So now they act!

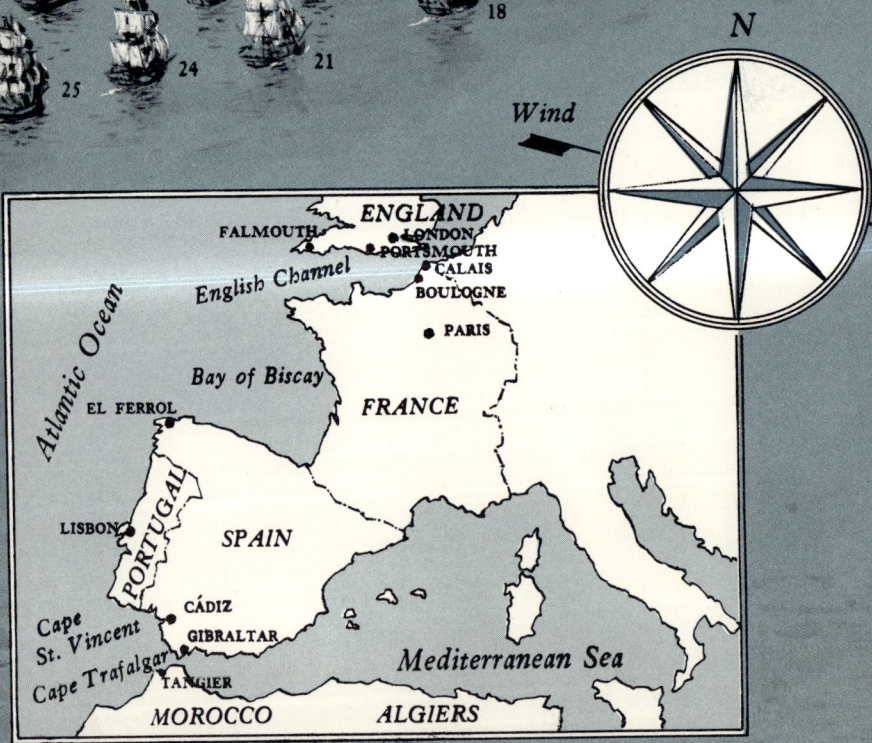

12

13

11 10 9 8 7 6 5 4 3 2 1

15
19 17 16 14
23 22 20 18
26
27 24 21
25
28

N

Wind

ENGLAND
FALMOUTH LONDON
PORTSMOUTH
CALAIS
English Channel BOULOGNE

PARIS

Bay of Biscay FRANCE

Atlantic Ocean

EL FERROL

PORTUGAL

LISBON SPAIN

Cape CÁDIZ
St. Vincent GIBRALTAR
Cape Trafalgar Mediterranean Sea
TANGIER
MOROCCO ALGIERS

THE TWO FLEETS

NOON, OCTOBER 21, 1805

★

BRITISH

Nelson's Division (12 of the line)

1	VICTORY	8	AGAMEMNON
	Nelson	9	ORION
2	TÉMÉRAIRE	10	MINOTAUR
3	NEPTUNE	11	SPARTIATE
4	LEVIATHAN	12	AFRICA
5	CONQUEROR		
6	BRITANNIA	13	EURYALUS
7	AJAX		(*frigate*)

Collingwood's Division (15 of the line)

14	ROYAL SOVEREIGN	21	REVENGE
	Collingwood	22	DEFIANCE
15	BELLEISLE	23	SWIFTSURE
16	MARS	24	POLYPHEMUS
17	TONNANT	25	DREADNOUGHT
18	BELLEROPHON	26	PRINCE
19	COLOSSUS	27	THUNDERER
20	ACHILLE	28	DEFENCE

FRENCH AND SPANISH

29	NEPTUNO—SP.	46	SANTA ANA—SP.
30	SCIPION—FR.	47	FOUGUEUX—FR.
31	INTRÉPIDE—FR.	48	MONARCA—SP.
32	FORMIDABLE—FR.	49	PLUTON—FR.
33	MONT-BLANC—FR.	50	ALGÉSIRAS—FR.
34	DUGUAY-TROUIN—FR.	51	BAHAMA—SP.
35	RAYO—SP.	52	AIGLE—FR.
36	SAN FRANCISCO	53	MONTAÑES—SP.
	DE ASIS—SP.	54	SWIFTSURE—FR.
37	SAN AUGUSTIN—SP.	55	ARGONAUTE—FR.
38	HÉROS—FR.	56	ARGONAUTA—SP.
39	SANTISSIMA	57	SAN ILDEFONSO—SP.
	TRINIDAD—SP.	58	ACHILLE—FR.
40	BUCENTAURE—FR.	59	PRINCIPE DE
	Villeneuve		ASTURIAS—SP.
41	REDOUTABLE—FR.		*Gravina*
42	SAN JUSTO—SP.	60	BERWICK—FR.
43	NEPTUNE—FR.	61	SAN JUAN DE
44	SAN LEANDRO—SP.		NEPOMUCENO—SP.
45	INDOMPTABLE—FR.		

★

CHAPTER THREE

BACKGROUND

IF IT WERE POSSIBLE to turn time back and fly over the scene in a helicopter, you would see a line of ships cut through the middle by a short line of other ships. Toward the rear of the long line, another short group has approached, on a converging angle. Several of these converging ships have cut through; others sail to get alongside rear ships in the long line, to fight them. Smoke drives before the light wind, hanging on the sea. Tall sails emerge here and there above the smoke clouds.

Away ahead of the long line, a squadron of ships sails slowly along, as if trying to get away. From them no cannon belch and no smoke rises. For the time being, they are not in the fight. But they seem to be turning, all together, swinging their yards and all their sails, slowly falling around from the direction of the wind on one side, bringing it on the other. It takes an hour to do this, for they go slowly in the slight wind. They come around at last, head back like creeping white haystacks toward the furiously fighting vessels.

Swooping low in your helicopter, you see that many of these are now damaged. Smoke billows high from fires in several. Masts topple. Some ships lie stopped. On others, men rush and fight with swords, cutlasses, tomahawks, on the deck, in hand-to-hand combat, boarders against defenders. From some ships come bursts of cheering. Here and there, in all the battle, ships' boats row about, saving men, picking up casualties, carrying messages.

A few of the big ships are heeling over, very slowly. But none capsizes. As yet, none sinks. Several ships are not in action at all. It all seems very slow.

Slow it might be, but this stately proceeding is vital. For so long as that Franco-Spanish fleet exists, or even the French part of it, Napoleon still has hopes of invading England.

Villeneuve Delays

Napoleon had already gathered huge forces once, a few weeks earlier, to make the attempt. In the summer of 1805, weeks before that fall day, he had assembled a great army under his best marshals, to invade England. At Boulogne, Ostend, Dunkirk, Calais, Étaples, and other seaside places stood 120,000 Frenchmen with an armada of 2,343 vessels, craft, barges, and boats, ready to swoop across the narrow channel on a 75-mile front. It was a wonderful army. Napoleon was a wonderful general. But he did not sail.

"If we can control the Straits for twelve hours, it is all up with England," he wrote.

But what about a navy to protect the invasion fleet during its vulnerable crossing?

Desperately, Napoleon thought of a midnight dash across that narrow channel to England.

"Only give me six hours!" he cried. One-fourth of one day's command of the narrow seas!

It was not to be his. Not then. Not ever.

For once, a fleet which might have done the job for him —Villeneuve's—was out, in the Atlantic somewhere. But news came that Villeneuve had sailed back to El Ferrol, a naval base on the northwestern coast of Spain, and thence to the strongly fortified port of Cádiz, almost a thousand miles from the place where his ships were wanted.

Once safely berthed in Cádiz Harbor, Villeneuve's French warships stayed there. With them was a strong squadron of Spanish vessels.

Napoleon fumed. But, for the moment at least, he could do nothing. After an impatient and futile wait, he had to withdraw his army. He had other immediate uses for it. Invasion plans must wait until the spring. The army could be assembled again; the invasion fleet would keep.

So Napoleon continued brilliantly with the kind of warfare he so thoroughly understood. The English, from their temporarily safe island, plotted to set up a strong alliance of anti-French Russians and Austrians at his rear, while the invasion army was pinned down at the Channel ports.

Napoleon heard of this. Swiftly he marched, caught the

Napoleon planned to use vessels like these to invade England.

Napoleon Bonaparte

Austrians unprepared at a place called Ulm, decimated them before a single Russian soldier could come to their aid.

Raging like a deadly and unconquerable lion across the mainland of Europe, Napoleon made one fatal mistake. He ordered the reluctant Admiral Villeneuve, still sheltered in the Spanish fortified port of Cádiz, to take his fleet to sea and make some contribution to the war effort with those costly, man-jammed floating fortresses.

He ordered the fleet into the Mediterranean, to ferry and support troops in some planned diversion there.

At first, Villeneuve did not obey these orders. He had a better sense of the strategic value of his ships than the landsman Napoleon. Besides, he knew Nelson. He had been one of the few senior officers to escape from the Battle of the Nile.

Bowsprit designs for the British ships Greyhound *and* Vigilant

The Spanish admirals in a council of war at Cádiz fully agreed with him. The risk was too great.

So week followed week and Villeneuve did not sail. Napoleon appointed another admiral to take over from him, a professional slight not to be taken lightly. Villeneuve heard of it. News traveled slowly, but faster than admirals. This was the last straw.

Before the new admiral could find coaches and horses swift enough to get him to Cádiz, Villeneuve sailed. At the moment, there was no sign of Nelson. He hoped against hope that he could reach the Mediterranean unseen.

Ships and Men

There was good reason for the French admiral to conserve his ships. He was no coward. His huge ships, bristling with their guns, were irreplaceable.

It had taken years to build those intricate, noble vessels—French, Spanish, English alike. No mass-production methods could fabricate such creations. Forests of old and well-grown oak, miles of hemp, acres of canvas, the skills of shipwrights, ironworkers, riggers, sailmakers, handed down through generations, must go into their construction. Stability, sailing qualities, fire power, and that strength to withstand the violent onslaughts of the raging sea which men call seaworthiness—these must be combined to perfection in the 100-gun ship-of-the-line.

The best of oak, long seasoned, worked laboriously, and shaped upon a massive keel of iron-hard elm, must form the stout hull. Enormous masts, so large around that no one tree could furnish them and they had to be built up of parts of huge trees expertly joined together, must "grow" in perfect symmetry from the hull—strong enough to stand up to gales, supported by a web of heaviest rope rigging, which, though it took up half the length of the ship on each side, must not obstruct the guns.

Model of a warship like those fighting in the Battle of Trafalgar

Since no tree and no made mast could be strong and high enough to rise from the ship's bottom to carry sufficient spread of sail, two other masts had to be built up as extensions of the first, the lower, mast—one above the other. The three formed a strong whole, supported by yet more cordage rigging, and carried the cross-spars called yards.

On these yards, the sails were set. Some were set—sheeted —by their lower corners down to the deck. Others were set to the extremities of the yards below them, and their own yards were then hoisted to give the sails maximum area and efficiency. In this manner, topsails were set above the principal sails, topgallant sails above them, and royals above all.

The whole complicated pattern of this array, which had grown up through slow and painful evolution down the sea centuries, was supported, controlled, and maneuvered by a series of apparently confused tackles, purchases, and long lengths of rope which snaked, twisted, and twined about the masts and yards like a spider's web, their ends falling to the deck in long ordered lines, there to be gathered around large wooden pegs called "pins." Each of the pieces of rope, no matter how small or large, had its name, its purpose, its own clear lead, and its own pin in convenient places around the masts and along the bulwarks.

Maintaining all this called for especially experienced and agile men by the dozen. Control and use of the sails called for courage and expertise long gone from the sea. If it took years to build the ships, it took many more years to learn to serve them, even longer to learn to handle one of them. The whole great fabric of masts, yards, rigging, and sails was contrived to accept and use the force of the wind (of any strength) from *behind* the sails only. A wind from ahead or bad handling which brought the wind from the wrong side (took the ship "aback," as sailors termed it) would cause immediate confusion and possible calamity.

Men risked their lives working such ships, even in the quietest weather on a peacetime cruise. The constant exercise of extreme vigilance by day and night was essential. Coolheadedness and the ability to size up a situation, make the right decision in a split second, and see it carried out were the qualities demanded of officers, as perfect knowledge of sailing seamanship, the alertness of a cat, and the endurance of a lion were required of the men.

Manning, maintaining, firing, and reloading the cumbersome guns called for similar care and knowledge. Above all, on the gun decks, the quarter-deck, the main deck, or aloft, efficiency depended upon good *spirit* and, with that, perfect drill. Imperfect gunnery could blast away precious powder and shot and achieve nothing. Slovenly reloading could nullify

The scene on a warship's quarter-deck during the heat of battle

Sailors today re-enact a grog line aboard the Victory.

the firing of a broadside. Indifferent maintenance could cause guns to blow up, killing their crews.

Drill, foresight, preparedness, and then drill and more drill again—these were the prerequisites for good seamen, good officers, good fighting ships.

Yet almost every aspect of life aboard frustrated the achievement of such standards. Intolerable living conditions were the rule, with harsh discipline. Floggings were frequent in too many ships. Poor food was accepted by hungry men. There was no shore leave at all while wars lasted (they went on for years), often little or no pay, and, for the crew, no pension.

Many of the men were "pressed." Sailors were seized out of homeward-bound merchantmen, slugged in waterfront dives and dragged aboard, stolen sometimes from their beds and forced to sea for years. Few volunteered for such a life.

But many of the pressed men were merchant seamen, hereditary sailing professionals of high quality and great ability in the handling of these complicated, demanding ships. A sailing merchantman was sailed the same way as a sailing warship. Since wars were fought—in essence—for merchantmen's protection and to make trade and merchant seafaring possible, there was some rough justice in it all. The young seaman was adaptable, easygoing, ready to accept his (to us) incredible life in a stout ship, in the company of good shipmates, under officers that he could respect for their ability and admire for their courage.

There were great satisfactions to be gained from his hard life, where the struggle with the elements was a personal challenge to the seaman—a challenge he knew he had to meet. The sailing-ship sailor's was a man's life, and red-blooded. In action there was the risk of quick death or maiming injury;

on the other hand, there might be prize money. Ships taken as prizes were sold, or assessed, and the prize money divided among the takers.

And after all, the grog flowed freely. Also, a seaman could have a "wife" aboard with him in every port, if he wanted, and no one would ask to see the marriage license.

A pressed seaman could rise in the navy, make a successful career of it if he were good enough and wanted to. At Trafalgar, *three-quarters* of the *Victory*'s seamen were pressed men, of twelve nationalities. More than seventy were not British. Both the first lieutenant and the signals officer had begun as pressed men and had risen from the ranks by their own worth and efforts.

Their way of life seems hard to us now because we enjoy better, in most ways. But for those seamen, perhaps it did not seem so hard, because it was for most the only life they knew.

As for the general run of officers, they had gone to sea as children, tossed from ocean to ocean and ship to ship from the age of eight or nine upward. They were midshipmen for seven years or more, then were promoted (if lucky or influential—preferably both) to lieutenant. With further good fortune, a lieutenant might leap to captain's rank in time of war in a few more years. Or he might never make it.

There were a few promoted seamen among them—but very few. Those with the king's commission came usually from the middle and so-called upper classes. To be an officer in the Royal Navy was a service of distinction, with hope of great reward—financial, from prize moneys; and glory, medals, and honors for service which came to notice in the proper quarters, even elevation to the peerage. Jack Tar, able seaman, might become in time Captain Sir John Tar, Baronet. Midshipman Tar could become Admiral the Earl of Tardom.

Twenty-seven Against Thirty-three

The British, as they join fiercely in that melee off Cape Trafalgar, have one great advantage, although outnumbered. They serve ships which have kept the sea. They attack ships which have been bottled up.

At sea, ships and seamen reach perfection. In port, both ships and men decay. Efficiency, fighting spirit, morale decline. Sailing ships on blockade duty must take risks to keep their stations. There is plenty of time for gun drill, for exercises aloft to bring sail-handling to perfection. In the daily exercise of their difficult calling, officers and men alike reach that standard of confident effectiveness which in violent hand-to-hand battle or murderous gun duel spells out the final victory.

Twenty-seven against thirty-three? Let them come!

A view of the battle shortly after the Victory *breaks the line*

★

CHAPTER FOUR

FIVE HOURS ONE MONDAY

HER SAILS SHREDDED by cannon balls but still effective, half the mizzenmast hanging over the side, all the studding sails and their booms on the foremast shot away, the greatest peril to Nelson's *Victory* came as she broke through the Franco-Spanish line. With both her broadsides fired away and her guns temporarily empty while five hundred men are frantically reloading, she glides into a knot of powerful enemy ships. Alone and for the moment unsupported, she ought to be shot out of the water. She is target number one, and her enemies can concentrate on her. No matter how good her gunners might be, three ships with 290 guns among them ought to be at least twice as good.

Just as she should never have been able to reach or to broach the line, she should have been destroyed after she did.

Those heavy guns, moving to firing positions on their clumsy carriages, have to be manhandled by tackles, spikes, and crowbars. They take time to reload. After a firing, the barrels must be thoroughly cleaned out lest any smoldering powder remain. If the smallest piece is left when the new charge is rammed in, the gun will explode in the men's faces.

French and Spanish ships fight back valiantly, violently. The *Bucentaure*, with Admiral Villeneuve aboard, fires four heavy broadsides before the *Victory* can reply with one— but what a one! Down come the French ship's main and mizzenmasts as the ship reels from the blow of the tons of hot iron exploded at her at point-blank range from the *Victory*'s double-shotted guns. Many gunners are killed. Guns are knocked off their carriages, flung on their sides. Brawny gunners, ten-year-old powder monkeys, shouting officers fall where they stand. Gun carriages out of control career about the rolling decks, mowing more men down, like clumsy bulldozers with no one driving them. On both sides, the huge, complicated web of heavy sails and rigging hangs outboard over gun ports, in part obscuring them, making it impossible for many gunners to see or for guns to be fired. The bodies of red-coated musketeers, tossed from the tops and mangled in their fall, roll into the sea. Fires start. Flames lick toward the powder trailing to the magazines.

As the *Bucentaure* reels, down comes the foremast too. Not a mast is left standing. The ship lies upon the sea rolling sluggishly, useless.

"My barge! My barge!" the French admiral shouts.

"Clear the admiral's barge!" the boatswain calls.

But the barge, although it has been made ready against such an emergency, is crushed beneath the wreckage of the masts.

Not a boat is available. The fallen rigging has destroyed them all.

An admiral in a dismasted ship is useless. The flag captain grasps a speaking trumpet. In a lull of firing, he hails the *Santissima Trinidad* to take the flagship in tow or to send a boat. No one in the flagship hears. They are fighting for their lives too.

Villeneuve is a prisoner in his own ship. Not so much as a spar is left to carry signals—if any other ships of the fleet had time to look at them or could see them in the smoke.

The Bucentaure Surrenders

Now the beautiful *Téméraire*, great English ship-of-the-line, ranges across the stern of the *Bucentaure*. Looking up, the French see her upper sails above the smoke. Her guns roar, belching death at the enemy ships at close quarters around her as she swings to the *Victory*'s support. At the same time, two French ships, the *Redoutable* and the *Neptune*, pour destructive fire into the *Victory* whenever they can see her. The *Redoutable*, closest, hooks together with the *Victory*, her lower guns touching the English ship's sides— so close that some French gunners, seeing the powder-stained, battle-savage faces of their fierce opponents staring at them 4 feet away, bang down the shutters of their gun ports and rush for the upper decks to continue the fight from there.

The dismasted, burning *Bucentaure* drifts slowly away, out of the thick of the fight. She has ceased firing. No one fires at her. There are enemies enough left to silence without wasting ammunition on a dismasted hulk. All her upper-deck and main-deck guns are abandoned, littered with dead and wounded thrown back in heaps, their bodies discolored by fire. Not enough fit men are left to carry the wounded away. On the main deck, things are worse. One dreadful shot, glancing along the beams of that low inferno just at head height, has knocked the heads from forty men.

The fleet astern of her is broken up, every ship fighting its own individual, desperate battle. The frigate detailed to attend the *Bucentaure* and repeat the admiral's signals is nowhere to be seen. A melee of three-deckers is no place for a small ship like a frigate—a lightly armed scout, not a heavy fighting ship.

Villeneuve himself is among the wounded, though—to his later regret—not seriously.

With not even his flag left to haul down, he waves a white handkerchief from the hammock nettings above the quarterdeck. It is enough. The surrender token is seen.

"The *Bucentaure* has played her part. Mine is not yet over," he declares. For a moment, he curses the fate which has so utterly frustrated him, then spared his life in the midst of so much slaughter.

A cutter, hastily launched, pulls nonchalantly across from another of Nelson's ships, the *Conqueror*, to accept the surrender of the *Bucentaure* and take her as prize, in accordance with the rules of sea war. In the cutter are Captain James

The Victory *tangles with the* Bucentaure (*painting by Turner*).

Warships of the two fleets battle valiantly up and down the line.

Atcherley of the *Conqueror*'s marines, a couple of seamen, a corporal, and two other marines. They do not know that the *Bucentaure* is the flagship.

The cutter secures to a lower step of the big ship's outboard ladder. Captain Atcherley clambers up. As his red coat shows above the nettings on the quarter-deck, he is astonished to see a tall, thin officer step forward, in the uniform of an admiral of the French navy. With him are two captains, as well as an officer in the resplendent uniform of a French general.

"To whom," asks the admiral, "have I the honor of surrendering?"

"To Captain Pellew of H.M.S. *Conqueror*," says the captain of marines, hastening to apologize for his own junior rank and assuring the distinguished group that he will find an officer more senior to accept their swords. This is the courtesy of the sea.

They go off in the little cutter, cannot find the *Conqueror* in the smoke (for she has moved off to fight another vessel), make instead for the *Mars*, and climb up the rolling sides, while the cannon roar.

But Captain Duff of the *Mars* has just been killed. Her first lieutenant, as the senior surviving officer, gravely accepts the admiral's and the general's swords for temporary safekeeping, to pass afterward to Lord Nelson.

So, in the midst of defeat and carnage, the rules of etiquette are observed.

An Exchange of Courtesies

Oddly enough, at the same time there is confusion about the surrender of the *Santissima Trinidad*. Because her capture means big money, every ship in the British fleet that day is eager to take her. The mighty four-decker is worth a fortune.

With her crew of 1,048 men and 138 guns, she is no easy prize. Through the long afternoon, she has fought on as

British ship after ship ranged close by, bashed broadsides into her, passed on to the next ship. She is too big to board, her upper decks inaccessibly high out of the water.

"The English shot tore our sails to shreds, as if huge talons had been tearing at them," reported the Spanish captain afterward. "Fragments of spars, splinters of wood, thick hempen cables cut up as corn is cut by the sickle, fallen blocks, shreds of canvas, bits of iron and hundreds of other things smashed off by the enemy's fire were piled about the deck. . . . Blood ran in streams, despite the sand. The rolling of the ship carried it about until it made strange patterns on the planks. . . . The ship creaked and groaned as she rolled. Through a thousand holes in the hull, the sea spurted in, flooding the hold."

In the middle of all this, shortly before the masts go, the smallest of the British ships, the 64-gun *Africa*, finds herself closest to the giant Spanish ship. With a burst of fire, the *Africa* adds further damage, shooting the Spanish flag away.

Instantly, Captain Digby lowers a boat, sends off a lieutenant named Smith to accept the captain's sword and the ship's surrender.

Lieutenant Smith climbs up the high outboard ladder on the ship's side. At the top, he is met by a group of officers with stately courtesy.

"But we have not surrendered, Señor Lieutenant," they explain. "We are getting up more ammunition. That is why firing has ceased for the moment."

It is an oversight that fresh colors have not been hoisted— an error put right at once as, with an exchange of proper naval courtesies, they see the crestfallen Lieutenant Smith, his hopes of big prize money blasted, overside and into his boat. Then the battle is on again.

The End of the Redoutable

Meanwhile, the *Victory*, locked together with the French *Redoutable*, continues fighting for her life. If the British did not know where the French admiral might be found, everyone on both sides knows where to look for Nelson.

The *Bucentaure* beaten into a hulk, the *Victory* faces the full force of the *Redoutable* and in part that of another French ship, the *Neptune*, as well. These are worthy opponents. Little Captain Lucas of the *Redoutable* (standing 4 feet 9 inches, about the size of a ship's powder monkey, a proper cock sparrow of a fighting man) has had his men trained to the utmost efficiency in the use of cutlass, pistol, grenades, musket, and bayonet, both to board and to repel boarders. They can throw grappling irons with the precision of an expert tennis player lobbing a ball over the net. Their fighting spirit is good, their morale excellent.

A cannon crew in action on the upper deck of a British warship

French vessels Redoutable *and* Bucentaure *fire on the* Victory.

At the height of the first stage of the battle, while only a few of the British ships have broken the French-Spanish line, the *Redoutable* makes ready to board the *Victory*. Hundreds of French, armed to the teeth, crowd the decks. Marines and soldiers toss grenades into the *Victory*'s upper decks or keep up musket fire from the tops and other vantage points in the rigging, mowing down gunners, signal men, powder monkeys, officers, marines.

The *Victory*'s upper deck is strewn with her dead, whose blood first trickles, soon streams in the sand.

"Away boarders! To the *Victory!*" comes the shout from aboard the *Redoutable*.

Hundreds of fierce seamen, cutlasses in teeth, grenades at the ready, leap for the rails. But they cannot board. The space between the two rolling ships is too great. No man can jump it. The French ship, too, is lower in the water. Her assault troops must leap upward as well as outward.

At the bow, there is a chance. These big ships carried awkward anchors, stuck out at both bows. French and British anchors lock together on one side. Instantly, Ensign Yon of the *Redoutable* scrambles over. A handful of seamen follow him. The *Victory* is immobile, her masts shot away. Aft on her quarter-deck, there is some distraction. Men are carrying off a body, fallen there on deck, the face draped with cloth.

The crew of the *Redoutable* rush to follow the brave ensign. But the *Victory*'s difficulties have not gone unnoticed by the *Téméraire*. Up she ranges, belts a mighty broadside into the French vessel, bangs her hull into the ship, knocks guns off their carriages and men from their feet with the impact, loads again, fires again.

Even five or six hundred men cannot mount hand-to-hand

The Redoutable *closes in as her men leap to the* Victory's *decks.*

combat and look to their guns too. The boarders tumble back to the *Redoutable* to load such guns as may still be fit for service, to blast back at the *Téméraire*. The *Victory*, for the moment forgotten, drifts slowly away. The *Téméraire* and *Redoutable* are so close that gun crews seize the ramrods from enemies' hands as they jump to clean their guns, firing their own guns inboard.

But the *Victory* cannot be entirely discounted. She too is getting up fresh ammunition. It is only the exposed upper deck which has suffered heavy casualties from French musket fire and grenades. The guns and the gun decks are all right. Within moments, she re-joins the battle.

As far as the *Redoutable* is concerned, all is over. Fire-eating Lucas can do no more. Of his 29 officers, 12 are dead, 10 badly wounded. He has lost 522 men from his ship's complement of 645, more than 300 of them dead, another 100 dying, the others too badly wounded to fight. Most of the survivors live only because they are working far below, in the storerooms and magazines, a few of them women, many boys. (Women sometimes went to sea—illegally, but tolerated —with their husbands in those times.) His masts have been shot away, his sharpshooting musketeers coming down with them. His rudder is blasted off, the entire afterpart of the ship smashed, almost every gun dismounted, capsized, or otherwise out of action. With hot shot still screaming into her, wounded are being killed as they lie helplessly in the cockpit, before the surgeons can get to them. The ship is leaking dangerously, the pumps destroyed, and she is afire.

All this within two hours of the battle's beginning.

The *Redoutable* surrenders.

No one comes to accept Captain Lucas' sword. He begins to fear that his ship will sink and take her wounded down with her. In the furious and violent mix-up continuing all around, no one pays attention to naval etiquette at that moment.

The *Redoutable* begins to settle in the water. The fire is under control, the leaks not.

For a while, four ships—the British *Victory* and *Téméraire*, the French *Redoutable* and *Fougueux*—are locked together, all dismasted or partially dismasted, all rudderless, out of control, all except the *Redoutable* still blasting mercilessly at each other.

Captain Lucas hails the *Téméraire*. "Come aboard and help us!" he shouts to the English ship.

The *Téméraire* is herself desperately engaged, her crew taking the *Fougueux* on her other side, by boarding. Not hearing, she makes no answer.

"Help us or I will set fire to the ship. We will all blow up together!" Captain Lucas shouts again.

This time the *Téméraire* hears, and she sends a party aboard, saves the wounded, rigs pumps. The *Téméraire*, *Redoutable*, and *Fougueux* remain locked together the rest of the long afternoon, both French ships surrendered and the *Téméraire* herself so damaged that she cannot break clear of them.

The *Victory*, mauled and partially dismasted as she is, still has her guns. She still is a fighting ship, though soon no longer able to maneuver much. Her enemies know her sting. They keep clear of her.

The *Redoutable* was so shot up that she sank the next day. She had gained one other distinction, as well as being one of the best-fighting French ships in the battle.

No one knew it at the time, but a musketeer firing from her mizzen-top had killed Lord Nelson.

★

CHAPTER FIVE

DEATH
OF A HERO

In battles between sailing ships, no one took shelter. On deck, there was none to take. The noncombatant surgeon worked far below in a steady part of the ship. A few old or partially crippled men passed up ammunition, also from far below. At these posts, they were most vulnerable to fire.

The rest, from admiral to youngest powder monkey, took what came.

Sailing ships had to be worked in the open. Sea fights had been fought from open or partially open decks since before the time of the ancient Greeks and Romans. Men had to see what they were doing. In 1805, combat in the end still was frequently hand to hand. Gunnery alone did not often suffice; cannon balls alone could not be relied on to do sufficient damage.

An admiral, too, had to see what his ships were doing. A captain could fight his ship from his quarter-deck, the place of authority, and from there alone.

The slaughter among officers was therefore great. At Trafalgar, Admiral Nelson headed the list of casualties. The captains of the *Mars* and *Bellerophon* also died, and four other British captains were seriously wounded. The French and Spanish suffered even worse. France's Rear Admiral Magon, the Spanish commodores Galiano and Churruca were all killed. The Spanish admiral Gravina was gravely wounded and later died of his wounds. Admiral Villeneuve, Vice-Admiral de Alava, Rear Admirals Cisneros and Escano, Commodores Infernet and Valdes were all wounded, all of them seriously, with the exception of Villeneuve, several more than once. Also, on the Franco-Spanish side, four captains were killed and nine others badly wounded. All these fell while fighting with the utmost bravery. Courage was not one-sided. Rear Admiral Magon, for example, was a French officer of noble birth who had been fighting at sea from the age of fourteen. Aboard the 74-gun *Algesiras* at Trafalgar, his hat and wig shot away, wounded in the right arm and shoulder, he was leading the crew in a rush to board the British *Tonnant* when a cannon ball struck him. It flung him onto the deck on his back, cut him almost in two.

The French commodore Infernet too had a long career of sea fighting and bravery. His midshipman son, aged ten, was with him in the *Intrépide* at Trafalgar. Father and son fought valiantly; their ship, almost totally dismasted, was the last to resist. Ten feet of water sloshed in the hold, and the sea was gaining steadily. Yet with half his crew dead or maimed, the commodore, severely wounded himself, had to be held down when the French colors were at last lowered.

Conspicuously dressed, officers led their men from prominent places, where they were expected to be. At such close quarters, they were easy targets. The more important officers were well-known to their enemies and easily recognized.

This applied to both sides—but to no one more than Nelson.

The Unmistakable Target

Admiral Nelson and Captain Hardy know very well about the sharpshooters up the French masts as they walk the *Victory*'s quarter-deck, from time to time calmly conversing, always watching the progress of the battle. Admiral Collingwood, in charge of the second line, and all the captains know what to do. There is no need for further direction.

The slight figure, in unmistakable admiral's uniform, with the empty right sleeve sewn across one breast adding further identification and the insignia of his four decorations boldly emblazoned on the other, invites sharpshooters' fire. The only wonder is that he lasted so long.

Up and down, up and down, the two officers stroll, their balance adjusted to the *Victory*'s motion. A little more than 40 feet away, a musketeer in the mizzen-topmast of the *Redoutable*, right alongside, rises, his musket ready. He has been firing at gunners and red-coated marines. Now another target offers itself. He takes quick aim. *Ping!*

The little admiral pitches forward on his face, shot down by the heavy ball. Entering through the left shoulder, it tears into his chest, smashing through the lungs and passing right through the spine.

"I trust," says the horrified Hardy, "that Your Lordship is not seriously wounded."

The still-conscious Nelson knows better. "They have done for me at last, Hardy," he gasps.

A sergeant of marines and two seamen run to him, lift him as tenderly as they can. Still calm despite the shock, the pain, the mortal wound, the admiral asks them to take out his handkerchief, cover his decorations and his face with it, so that his sailors will not see who it is that is being carried below.

The Surgeon's Cockpit

The admiral is no stranger to the shambles of the surgeon's cockpit or the searing sting of his knife. He has been severely wounded in other actions.

Above his head, the gun carriages trundle and the guns thunder, for the *Victory* remains in the thick of the fight.

Around the dying admiral, sailors moan in the delirium of intolerable pain.

Man after man is laid upon the dreadful table, hacked, probed, sawn. A quick look at Nelson's wound shows the surgeon that it is mortal.

"Mr. Beatty, you can do nothing for me," the admiral says. "The blood gushes every minute in my chest. I felt the bullet break my back."

Nelson is felled by a musketeer's bullet (painting by Dighton).

Now and again a burst of British cheering, heard from the open gun ports, tells of yet another French or Spanish ship surrendered.

Captain Hardy has taken over the conduct of the battle. The *Victory* is still the senior ship. All others look to her for signals, when they can see her. Vice-Admiral Collingwood, fighting valiantly with his line against 17 enemies, knows nothing of Nelson's fate, though a boat is already hurrying across the water to bring him the news.

At last, Hardy has time to rush quickly below. He is an old friend and shipmate of Lord Nelson, as well as his flag captain.

"How goes the battle, Hardy?"

"Very well, my Lord. We have twelve or fourteen of the enemy's ships in our possession."

"That is well; but I bargained for twenty. . . . Don't throw me overboard, Hardy. And take care: a gale is coming up. Anchor the fleet when you can."

A little later he is heard to thank God that he has done his duty.

The admiral was struck down at 1:25 P.M. At half-past four, he died.

"Firing continued until 4:30," the *Victory*'s log tersely records, "when, a victory having been reported to the Right Hon. Lord Viscount Nelson, K.B., and Commander-in-Chief, he died."

4:30 P.M.

By coincidence, though none outside the *Victory*'s cockpit (and very few there) know of the admiral's death, the battle ceases at that precise moment; all the separate fights, the ter-

The death of Lord Nelson, October 21, 1805 (painting by Devis)

rible duels, the bloody, sword-wielding boarding parties and their furious affrays come to an end; all stops, vanquished and victors alike worn out by their efforts.

By coincidence too, and not by plan, a ring of great ships has gathered; the rolling, partly dismasted *Victory* in the center, the others in a rough circle around her. Smashed and shot-away masts, broken spars, torn sails trail from them. Jagged stumps of masts stand from the decks, and yards roll in the sea.

The wind gets up, and it cries in such rigging as still is left with the moaning increase of coming storm. The sea also rises. Without windage in their sails to steady them, the battered, bruised, and tormented hulls roll heavily. Blood gushes from scuppers. Sea squelches into them through their wounds. Torn bodies drift on the swirling waters. A French ship, the *Achille*, burns furiously, the billowing smoke blowing over the ring of the dismasted ships, like a funeral pyre.

Over every ship in sight flies the British flag, sometimes above the Spanish, sometimes the French, most frequently alone.

Not a single British ship has surrendered, though some have been fought to a standstill. Like sullen, huge bull whales, they lie almost awash upon the surface of the sea, waiting, licking their wounds, for the moment silent in the aftermath. It is as if the ships themselves were aware of Nelson's passing —and know that no such ships will ever see his like again.

With a frightful blast heard as far away as Cádiz and a bursting roar of overwhelming flame, the burning *Achille* blows up. Vivid flames shoot skyward and billow, for a few seconds, into a ball of fire, darkened with the spots of broken timbers and broken bodies flung skyward with it. Men gaze in awe, breathe a silent prayer.

Down sinks the *Achille*, still in flames, her French flag flying. Many of her brave crew go down with her.

She is the eighteenth of the 33 French and Spanish ships lost this day; 17 have surrendered, not 14 as Hardy counted— 18 out of 33 fought from the sea by the 27 British.

This is a very great victory indeed, accomplished by the

The regal wreckage of the two fleets at the climax of the battle

*Admiral Don
Federico Gravina*

British under Lord Nelson in less than five hours that Monday afternoon, without losing a single ship themselves. More than that, the British have achieved their victory at the cost of 449 killed, while the French alone have lost 3,000 killed and 1,000 wounded.

Only 15 Franco-Spanish ships escaped, some scarcely having fought at all. None of these will fight again. The Spanish admiral Gravina, leading a squadron of 11 ships toward Cádiz, is himself mortally wounded. At Cádiz, he learns of the death of Nelson.

"I am a dying man, but I die happy!" he declares upon his deathbed. "I am going, I hope and trust, to join Nelson, the greatest hero the world has produced!"

CHRONOLOGY

OCTOBER 21, 1805, 6:00 A.M. Daylight off Cape Trafalgar reveals the opposing fleets, the 33 French and Spanish, 27 English ships-of-the-line. The English are to seaward, sailing in two divisions—one (12 ships) under the Commander-in-Chief, Vice-Admiral Viscount Nelson, the other (15 ships) under his second-in-command, Vice-Admiral Collingwood. The Franco-Spanish fleet is in one long line, under Commander-in-Chief Vice-Admiral Pierre Silvestre de Villeneuve of the French navy; it heads slowly toward the Strait of Gibraltar. Wind light, west-northwest; heavy swell from westward, after a windy night, but decreasing.

6:05 A.M. Led by the *Victory*, the English ships set all possible sail and head toward the Franco-Spanish.

6:40 A.M. Nelson signals "Prepare for battle." Ships clear for action, the two English columns about a mile apart. Nelson heads on a converging course, apparently sailing toward the leading enemy ships.

8:30 A.M. Franco-Spanish fleet alters course 180 degrees to head back toward base at Cádiz. Nelson swings his two columns after them to force battle; he still "feints" toward the leading ships, although he does not intend to attack them. The Franco-Spanish ships clear for action.

10:30 A.M. Wind dropping, swell decreasing. Nelson alters course to cut across the Franco-Spanish line at its center, by the great ship *Santissima Trinidad*. He is looking for Villeneuve's ship, but the French leader shows no distinctive flag. He is, in fact, aboard the *Bucentaure*.

11:00 A.M. Nelson, in his cabin, writes his famous prebattle prayer: "May the Great God whom I worship grant to my country, and for the benefit of Europe in general, a great and glorious victory; and may no misconduct in anyone tarnish it; and may humanity after victory be the predominant feature in the British Fleet. For myself, I commit my life to Him who made me, and may His blessing light upon my endeavours for serving my country faithfully. To Him I resign myself, and the just cause which is entrusted to me to defend. Amen. Amen. Amen."

11:35 A.M. Nelson hoists the signal "England expects that every man will do his duty."

"What is Nelson signalling about?" asks Collingwood. "We know well enough what we have to do." The fleet answers with cheers. . . . Villeneuve, pointing out the bold manner in which both Nelson and Collingwood lead their columns into action, exclaims, "Nothing but victory can attend such gallant conduct."

NOON. The two fleets are closing. The French try the range. Their shots fall short. The French ship *Fougueux* opens up on Collingwood's *Royal Sovereign*, which is closer to the rear of the enemy line than Nelson is to the center. The center has sagged to leeward; Nelson must sail a little further yet.

12:10 P.M. The *Royal Sovereign* passes through the enemy's line between the *Santa Ana* and the *Fougueux*, giving each a broadside. The battle proper at last begins, but in the light wind, it is another fifteen minutes before Collingwood's second ship can sail into action.

12:20 P.M. The center French ships find their range—400 guns open up on the *Victory* as she continues to sail slowly toward them. As yet, she cannot answer.

12:40 P.M. The *Victory*'s mizzenmast is shot in two and her steering wheel smashed. Shots crash through her sails, which are soon in shreds. The wind has almost died away, but the *Victory* ghosts on.

12:59 P.M. The *Victory* breaks the line, at last is able to reply; her first salvo, into the stern of Villeneuve's flagship *Bucentaure*, wrecks the whole stern and 20 guns, kills and wounds 400 men. The ships pass so close that the *Victory*'s yards tangle with the *Bucentaure*'s rigging. At the same time, the French ship *Redoutable*, ably fought by Captain Lucas, heavily attacks the *Victory* at close range. "In attempting to pass through the Enemy's Line fell on board the 10th and 11th Ships of the Enemy's Line when the Action became General," writes the *Victory*'s master, Thomas Atkinson, in his log.

1:30 P.M. Nelson has brought on the melee. The battle becomes a wild mix-up of furiously tangled fighting ships. Each ship knows only the events immediately concerning itself. . . . Sharpshooters in the *Redoutable*'s tops cause heavy casualties on the *Victory*'s upper decks. One of them hits the admiral, who pitches to the deck. "They have done for me at last, Hardy," he gasps, and he is carried below.

2:00 P.M. Guns roar, gun carriages trundle furiously above the dying admiral's head, punctuated by the cheers of seamen as enemy ship after ship, fought to a standstill, strikes her flag and surrenders.

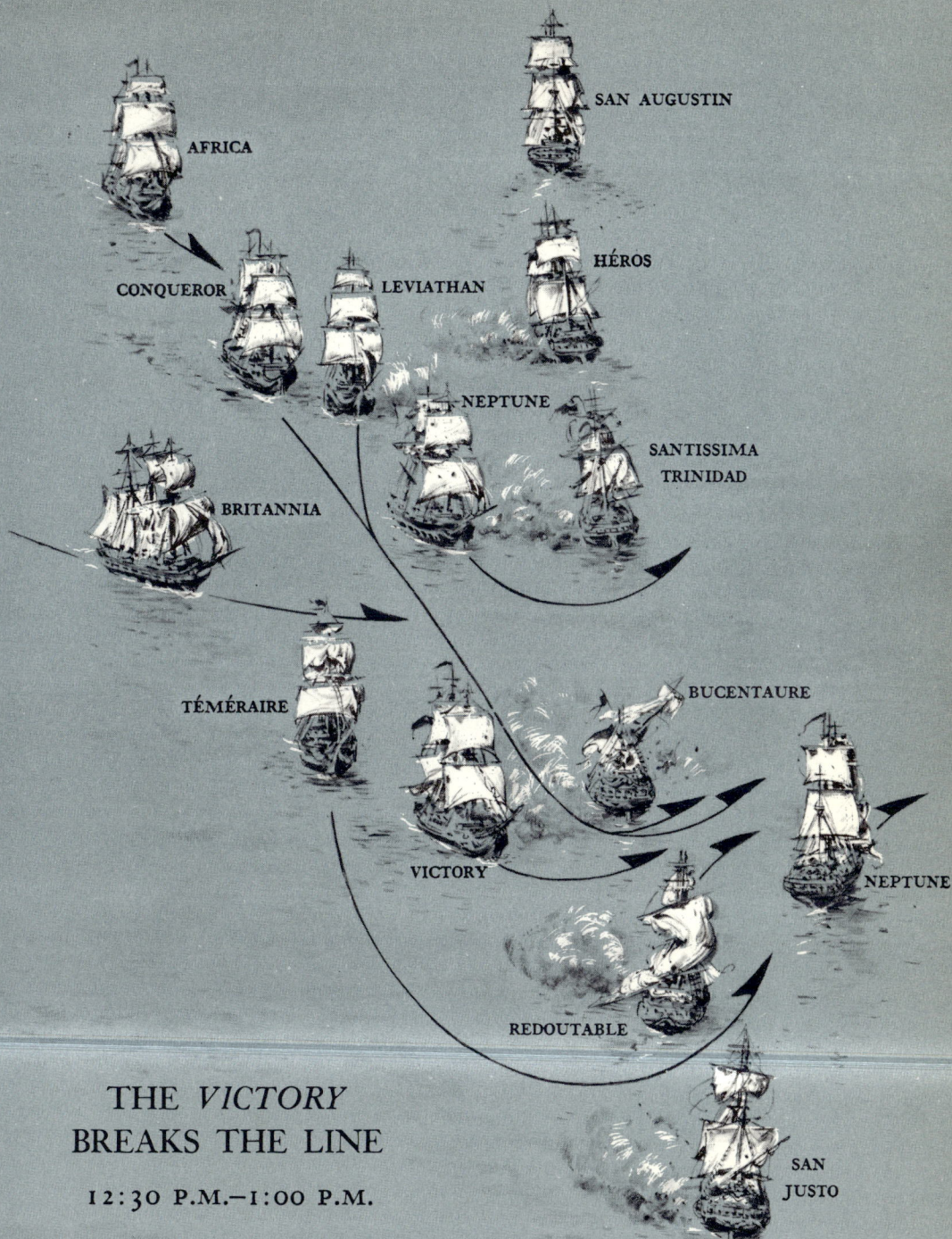

AFRICA

SAN AUGUSTIN

CONQUEROR

LEVIATHAN

HÉROS

NEPTUNE

BRITANNIA

SANTISSIMA
TRINIDAD

TÉMÉRAIRE

BUCENTAURE

NEPTUNE

VICTORY

REDOUTABLE

SAN
JUSTO

THE *VICTORY*
BREAKS THE LINE

12:30 P.M.—1:00 P.M.

3:00 P.M. The battle is at its height; more and more of the British ships sail into action, falling upon the enemy's center and rear. Some of the Franco-Spanish ships ahead turn slowly back to help their comrades—too late. The *Victory* is badly mauled, her rigging cut to pieces, her upper decks filled with dead, dying, and seriously wounded, her oak hull pounded by a thousand heavy shot fired at the closest quarters.

Seven of her officers are dead, eight more seriously wounded.

3:35 P.M. The battle quietens; most of the individual ship duels are over. A few Franco-Spanish ships of the leading section, sailing slowly back, get a hot reception and turn away. The *Victory*'s captain has time to visit the dying Nelson, deep in the cockpit. "The victory is complete," he reports. . . . "We have twelve or fourteen of the enemy's ships in our possession." "That is well," says Nelson, "but I bargained for twenty." (In fact, seventeen had surrendered. A little later, an eighteenth blew up.)

4:30 P.M. "Having for some time ceased to suffer . . . Nelson ceased to breathe," records the *Victory*'s log. At this moment, the main battle also ceases. A few stragglers fight on ineffectually.

5:30 P.M. Last shot is fired. All fighting is over. Crews begin at once to repair damage, rerig their ships, set fresh sail, prepare for approaching storm.

★

Postscript

JUNE, 1848. Government of Great Britain awards a Trafalgar medal to seamen and marine survivors of the battle. (Previously only captains and admirals had received gold medals.)

APRIL, 1912. Lords Commissioners of the Admiralty appoint a committee "for the purpose of thoroughly examining and considering the whole of the evidence relative to the tactics employed by Nelson at the Battle of Trafalgar."

JULY 17, 1913. Report completed and published.

The War with the Sea

The battle between the ships is over; but now another conflict in the endless war of men with the sea is about to begin. The storm which has been rising is blowing in from the Atlantic. On one side of the ships, only a few miles away, are the shoals off Cape Trafalgar and the wild coast of Spain; on the other, the breadth of the stormy ocean. They drift toward the shoals.

Battered ships are in no state to keep the sea and fight the storm. Battered men, their mouths filled with the pungent taste of powder and of blood, run to deal with leaks, stanch their ships' wounds, get auxiliary steering gear working, contrive on stumpy masts a measure of sail at least sufficient to blow their ships before the wind toward Gibraltar. Rowboats put out from less damaged vessels to pick up survivors from the tangled flotsam of corpses, broken spars, and rent timbers floating everywhere. Friend and foe alike are plucked from the churning waters if there seems a chance that there is life left in them.

Extraordinary features mark this search. At least two survivors picked up are young Frenchwomen, both of whom had been in the thick of the battle. One of these, whose name is recorded only as Jeannette, is from the *Achille*. She is picked up naked, suffering from exposure and from burns. Her husband had been aboard, she said; she had joined him (as other women on both sides also did), disguised as a man.

In the battle, she handed up powder from one of the big magazines. The fire in the *Achille* trapped her below. Beginning above, the fire ate downward, destroying the companionways, which were the only means of escape. At last, she was alone. She watched the guns of the deck above come crashing through the burned planks, saw the flames licking toward the magazines. She ripped off her clothes, leaped through an open gun port into the sea.

But she could not swim. Grasping the rudder chains, she pulled herself to the rudder. Then the fire melted the leaden lining of the rudder trunk. Molten lead fell, sizzling in the sea. It began to fall on her. She had to let go. A small plank drifted near. She grabbed that, but it could scarcely support her. A French seaman, seeing her there, brought a larger plank and switched with her. Burned about the neck and chest, smoke begrimed, and powder blackened, she has been in the water for two hours.

A boat from the *Defence* picks her up at last. The seamen pool their shirts to clothe her. Aboard, one of the lieutenants gives her his cabin. The next day, to her indescribable joy, she finds her husband, also a prisoner aboard. When the ship reaches Gibraltar, both are freed.

At least one other woman is picked up from the *Achille*.

How many women, on both sides, took part in the battle will never be known. There were some also in the British ships, probably quite a number. Their names do not appear on the books. Though officially allowed aboard by the hundreds in port, they were stowaways at sea, hidden with the connivance of the crew, their presence unknown to the officers. With so many very young boys in the crew, a slim girl in the seaman's rough shirt, trousers, scarf, and kerchief of those days might pass muster along the dark mess decks. When the drums beat to quarters, they too slipped quietly to unobtrusive action stations.

As for boys of nine and ten years old, their small bodies tossing in the sea were taken as a matter of course.

The gale rose, as Nelson foresaw it would. Many of the 27 British ships and all their 17 surviving prizes were now alike in peril.

As the cannon smoke clears, gale winds blow in off the Atlantic.

CHAPTER SIX

AFTERMATH

"I WOULD RATHER FIGHT another battle than pass again through such a week as followed it," later wrote the English admiral Collingwood of the storm which followed Trafalgar. For more than a week, the gale blew violently. Five of the Spanish and French prizes sank, including the *Santissima Trinidad*. Nine drove ashore or onto shoals, where the sea tore them to pieces.

To be able to fire their guns at all, warships had to open long lines of ports, hinged lids cut through their sides in rows. Such lids were lowered and closed in hard weather. Never wholly watertight, battle damage knocked them off or caused them to leak.

As the ships rolled, more sea gushed in through all these leaks and defective ports, sloshing across the decks, pouring into the hold. From there, it was pumped out by hand with inefficient suction pumps, themselves for the most part damaged. As more and more sea came in, the ships settled lower, until more water came in than could be pumped out. Then they sank.

When the storm began, the men were battle weary, many of them wounded. There could be no thought of a warm meal. The French and Spanish were further dispirited by defeat and their fate as prisoners. English crews fought to save the ships, not only their own but the French and Spanish as well. A sunken enemy paid no prize money. To make a bad situation worse, the heavy fall gale continued day after day, driving the unmanageable ships steadily toward the coast of Spain. A ship blown ashore in a raging sea stands no chance; for the sea then, finding an impediment in its path, smashes right over it, lashing at it, crashing at it, but never driving it close enough inshore for men to survive. The deep keel snarls with the offshore rocks or the shoals well out, and men cannot swim or survive in the violent surf. Indeed, few of these sailors could swim, at any time. Swimming was not encouraged.

From the *Santissima Trinidad*, a survivor later gave a vivid picture of her last scenes: "The winds and waves tossed and buffeted our ship in their fury. . . . The rolling was so terrible that it was very difficult even to work the pumps. . . . An English vessel, the *Prince*, tried to take us in tow, but . . . she was forced to keep off for fear of a collision which would have been fatal to both. . . . On one side, covered with the Spanish flag, lay the bodies of the officers who had been killed. They alone aboard the *Trinidad* really knew rest."

After four days, the great ship had to be abandoned. It was obvious that she must soon go down. In the horrible sea, boats from the *Prince* fought their way between the two ships, ferrying survivors across—first the wounded, then the others.

"We had to tie the poor mangled wretches round the waists or where we could, and lower them into a tumbling boat beneath the stern—some without arms, others with no legs. . . . The sea was now sweeping over the main deck, the weather dark and the hurricane still blowing. Our superb ship could not last another ten minutes."

The frightening, violent uproar of the tossing sea was endless and terrible, as if the ocean were determined to finish the
destruction which men had begun. Huge raging seas hurled
themselves at the floundering hulls of wounded ships. Many
ships were all but awash, like half-tide rocks, with spray,
spume, and the top of the sea itself driving at them, all around
them, over them. The gale screamed in such rigging as survived, adding its alarming, ceaseless sound to the general
terror.

Yet in all these ships, men worked on, heroically and without rest.

Every British vessel survived to reach Gibraltar, but it
took a week. The direct distance from off Cape Trafalgar
was about 50 miles. Of the 17 enemy prizes still afloat after
the battle, the British managed to save only 4.

In the meantime, the French rear admiral Dumanoir, es-
caping with 4 practically unfought survivors, sailed into a
British squadron from the Channel fleet, under Sir Richard
Strachan. All 4 were captured. The French ships which

A French frigate, Themis, *hauls the* Santa Ana *back to Cádiz.*

The battle-ravaged Victory *is towed past the Rock of Gibraltar.*

sailed with Admiral Gravina into Cádiz never fought for France again. They were blockaded until 1808, when Spain rose against Napoleon and seized them.

The Pickle *Makes for England*

At Cádiz itself, while the battle raged that Monday afternoon, the citizens heard the roar of the guns and saw the smoke. The thundering noise rolled inland over half Andalusia and among the rich orange and cork groves of Medina-Sidonia. As far off as Tangier, people rushed to hilltops to see the dark smudge in the sky and to listen with awe to the terrific bellowing of the cannon.

"Ten days after the battle, they were still employed here bringing the wounded ashore," wrote an Englishman at Cádiz late that October. "The wounded were carried away to hospitals, convents, churches, in every shape of human misery, while crowds of Spaniards assisted or looked on with horror. Their companions who had escaped unhurt wandered the streets with folded arms and downcast eyes. . . . As far as the eye could reach, the sandy side of the isthmus was covered with masts and yards, the wrecks of ships, and here and there the bodies of the dead. . . . In the ocean, at a distance, masts and parts of ships floated about. The sea was now calm . . . yet not a boat ventured out, so great still was their apprehension of the enemy. . . . Piles of the dead washed ashore with every tide. . . ."

Meanwhile, the fast schooner *Pickle*, a messenger ship for the fleet, was fighting her way the thousand miles from Trafalgar toward England with the news of the victory. It was five days before Collingwood had a chance to write anything, as he was fighting to save first his own ships, then the prizes. The *Pickle* sailed on October 27th—the very day, by chance, that England learned of Napoleon's victory over the Austrians at Ulm. (The French had sent out an empty boat from Boulogne to drift toward England with the staggering news.)

On November 4th, eight days later, the *Pickle* was off Falmouth in Cornwall, at the Atlantic end of the English Channel. Rushed ashore by boat before the schooner was anchored, the *Pickle*'s captain set out for London, Admiral Collingwood's satchel of dispatches on his back. It is the best part of 290 miles from Falmouth to London; even with the swiftest horses, the journey took another two days, two nights, and 19 mounts.

Galloping to the gates of Admiralty in the post chaise in which he finished the trip, with a clatter of wheels and iron hooves on cobbles, the lieutenant leaps out, runs inside. It is one o'clock in the morning, November 6, 1805.

Mr. Marsden, First Secretary of the Board of Admiralty, is

still at work by the light of his tall wax candles, in the fitful warmth of his dying fire.

A sharp knock: in comes the *Pickle*'s captain, dressed as he landed from that small schooner, travel stained, and tired.

"Sir," he announces without delay, "we have won a great victory, but we have lost Lord Nelson!"

Taking the dispatches and one of the candles, the First Secretary hurries to awaken the First Lord, eighty-year-old Admiral Lord Barham. Such vital news must be made known at once.

Drawing aside the bed curtains by the light of the candle, the Secretary awakens the old peer from his sound slumbers.

"What is the news, Mr. Marsden?" he asks, very quietly, and is quietly told.

In the morning, everyone knows. The shock of the death of Nelson affects the people far more than the news of his victory. While in the press offices type is hand-set to spell out the news, crowds clamor at the doors. They ask no details of the victory. Is it true, they want to know, about Lord Nelson?

At Windsor Castle, even George III is silent for some minutes when he learns. The queen, with her princesses around her, hears the dispatch read out with him. They all burst into tears.

Later that day, an empty boat is let go just off the French side of the Channel, to drift into Boulogne. This time the boat is English, not French. In it are copies of the *Government Gazette*, with the news of Trafalgar.

France had hushed it up. Napoleon's land victories at Ulm and Austerlitz were useful diversions, for the time being.

But no army came again to the Channel ports hoping to conquer England.

Nelson's funeral procession leaves Greenwich on January 8, 1806.

The Consequences of Trafalgar

Nelson and his captains had done more than annihilate a fleet. They had crushed French naval strength for the remainder of the Napoleonic Wars. Compelled to write off his navy, Napoleon continued his sweeping land campaigns. Although he won victory after victory ashore, his end began to appear as inevitable. With no hope of control of the sea, he was lost.

To Napoleon, Trafalgar was an irrevocable disaster.

Without an effective navy, he was cut off, pinned to Europe, while Britain, with undisputed mastery of all the seas, could build up world trade and prosper. Not only was the French plan of cross-channel invasion rendered impossible —the whole area of French conquest was blockaded. Such French warships as survived or were built up again became floating barracks, swinging to their anchors uselessly in harbor, not daring to go to sea, using man power to no purpose, gaining neither sea nor war experience.

French merchant ships, the life line of trade, suffered more. In a space of ten years, the British captured 1,250 of them that were either trying to scamper into port from some short voyage or sneaking out to begin one. In this same time, the merchant fleet of Britain increased by 6,000 ships.

With such fleets of warships and merchantmen, Britain became the richest and most powerful country in the world. Moneys earned from her unhindered trade helped to finance anti-French alliances, which in the end were bound to bring Napoleon's conquests to nothing. This is what Nelson had foreseen in his determination to annihilate the French fleet. His decisive victory at sea gave hope to all in the overrun countries.

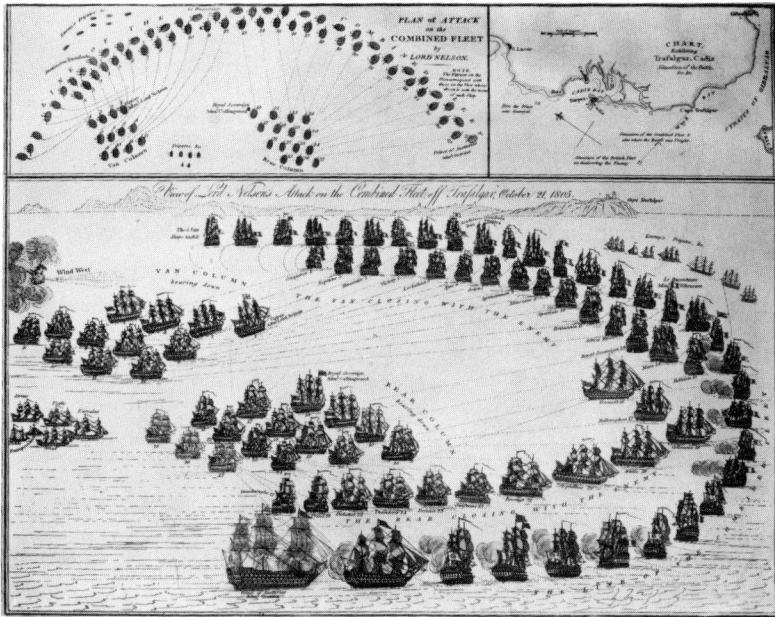

Diagram of Admiral Nelson's plan of attack against Villeneuve

Beginning with Spain, Europe rose against Napoleon. Trafalgar was fought in 1805. It was 1815 before the French land armies were crushed finally at the Battle of Waterloo, but long before that their real power had gone from them.

The great American seaman and sea historian Alfred Mahan wrote later that the defeats of Napoleon at "Moscow and Waterloo are the inevitable consequences of Trafalgar."

As far away as India and the newly founded Australia (its first British settlement was only seventeen years old in 1805), the results of Nelson's victory brought fresh hope to men. French naval officers had been sailing to Australia, looking for Pacific bases there. French hopes of dominating the rich trade of the Indian Ocean spelled no good to any land but Napoleonic France. All such hopes, too, dispersed in the smoke of the cannon at Trafalgar.

Apart from the brief War of 1870 Napoleon's defeat at Waterloo was followed by a state of peace and settled living in Europe for the following hundred years. Trade routes spread, and the Industrial Revolution flourished. Across the Atlantic, the United States—not much older than Australia when Admiral Nelson died—grew from the thirteen original states to a mighty, coast-to-coast nation, powerful and prospering.

The Greatest Admiral in the World

Just how and why was Nelson so outstanding an admiral? Just what was his magic? There had been other great admirals and sea victories before him, many of them. He had defects, as everybody has. He was vain. He loved glory. He could be a fool with women. He had made a mess of his private life and, for these and other reasons, was unpopular in some quarters in England. Though a captain of distinction at twenty, he had to wait for his turn, through slow seniority, to reach the rank of vice-admiral. He was never specially promoted.

Though no officer ever fought at sea more valiantly or cleverly or with such overwhelming success, the high honors which might have been his were not awarded him. Of the four bright stars on the vice-admiral's uniform in which he died, only one—the Order of the Bath—was English. He was a duke, but of Bronte in Sicily—a dukedom given him by a king in Italy and not in England. In the land of his birth, he was a viscount, a title which is also by courtesy bestowed on earls' eldest sons and ranks between a baron and an earl. All barons, viscounts, and earls are commonly called lords, but by no means rate the same.

Nelson was a magnificent fighting seaman, and he was

Lord Nelson, the world's greatest admiral (portrait by Abbott)

aware of it. Such awareness in another might have been offensive. It is a measure of his greatness that brother officers, with few exceptions, accepted it. He was outstanding both as strategist and as tactician. He did not just win battles by ingenious tactics. First, by mastery of the science of naval warfare, he *made battles happen,* under conditions of greatest possible advantage to his side. He led confident men who could press the advantage.

Above all, Nelson was that great and most rare person, a gentle man, warmhearted, human, and humane. His men loved him. His officers worshiped him. He inspired both alike to put forward their greatest efforts no matter what the odds, just because they knew he was leading them. Perhaps they liked him more because some landsmen in high quarters liked him less.

He had the aura of success. He believed in his men, his ships, his officers. Above all, he believed in his captains, that "band of brothers" (as he called them) ready to follow him anywhere, anyhow, at any time, even to their deaths. Some of them had been with him before, in other battles, but by no means all. Collingwood had been the first to swing out of the line to his support in the Battle of Cape St. Vincent, where— not for the first time—Nelson's defiance of precise and traditional orders was of the greatest value in bringing victory to the English.

At Trafalgar, only 8 of the 27 British captains had served with Nelson before; only 5 had previously commanded a ship-of-the-line in battle. Two ships were fought by their youthful first lieutenants, for their captains—to their disgust —had been recalled to England to attend some court of inquiry. But they all knew Nelson and his marvelous reputation, and they knew that, with him, they were bound to win.

Unanswered Questions

Two mysteries remain. Correctly foreseeing Nelson's tactics, why did Villeneuve do nothing to counteract them? While Nelson and Collingwood sailed so slowly toward his unwieldy line that long morning, for what possible reason did he maintain the line and thus await its decimation and his own defeat?

Only Vice-Admiral Villeneuve himself could provide the answer. He never did. He died in France, apparently by his own hand, not long after the battle—an exchanged prisoner, unemployed, unwanted, an admiral without a fleet.

To the other mystery, there is no answer either. Did Nelson openly seek his own death? He certainly foresaw it; he spoke of it to his captains. He did nothing to avoid it. He was well aware of the French sharpshooters, yet neither posted snipers

A ship's sextant

The Victory, *symbol of the age of fighting sail, at Portsmouth*

of his own to pick them off nor took any other precaution. Target number one and knowing it, he advertised himself quite openly for more than one hour, within yards of French sharpshooters seeking to destroy him. It was tactfully hinted to him that he might change his jacket and wear one without the embroidered insignia of his four decorations. He declined.

Nelson had placed his affairs in order, written his last prayer, prepared himself for his end as far as a man is able. But so had others who were also in great danger.

The very completeness of the victory, which he never doubted, would have one effect which his remarkably clear mind must have foreseen. It would leave him without further work to do, leave England with no need of his services. In whatever life span might remain to him, there would be no more naval enemies to destroy.

What then was left for him? To live on for years, an unemployed sea dog, an embarrassing hero? No, better a dead hero, killed among his seamen, his friends, and the ships he loved, in his last great victory. . . .

God knows. Perhaps not even Nelson himself could give any real answer.

"Band of Brothers"

During the Second World War, from 1939 to 1945, when for some time Britain was again at bay and alone held out against a temporarily successful dictator gone mad in Europe, British admirals, commodores, and captains kept always one talisman, one ubiquitous object of inspiration in their cabins:

It was a statuette or a painting of Lord Nelson.

More than 130 years after Trafalgar, they were still his captains.

CROSS SECTION OF H.M.S. *VICTORY*

Built to the design of Sir Thomas Slade, her keel was laid down at the Old Single Dock, Chatham, on July 23, 1759, and she was launched on May 7, 1765. Cross-section drawing by Colin Mudie.

1	POOP	9	GANGWAY
2	HAMMOCK NETTINGS	10	FO'C'SLE
3	MIZZENMAST	11	CARRONADES
4	QUARTER-DECK	12	FOREMAST
5	STEERING WHEELS	13	HARDY'S CABIN
6	HERE NELSON FELL	14	UPPER DECK
7	PIKES	15	NELSON'S DAY CABIN
8	MAINMAST	16	NELSON'S DINING CABIN

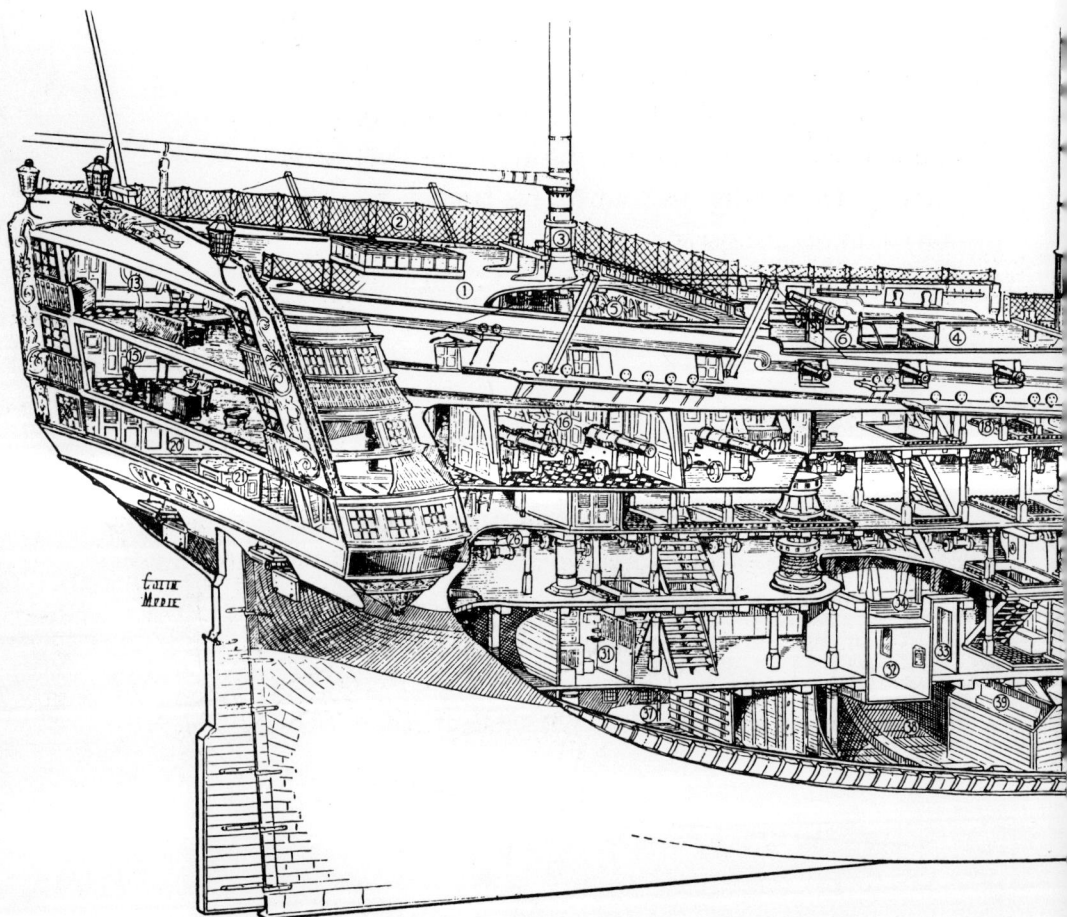

17	NELSON'S SLEEPING CABIN	31	SICK BAY
18	SHOT GARLANDS	32	AFT HANGING MAGAZINE
19	MIDDLE DECK	33	LAMP ROOM
20	WARDROOM	34	HERE NELSON DIED
21	TILLER HEAD	35	FORWARD HANGING
22	ENTRY PORT		MAGAZINE
23	CAPSTAN HEAD	36	POWDER STORE
24	GALLEY AND STOVE	37	POWDER ROOM
25	LOWER DECK	38	AFT HOLD
26	TILLER	39	SHOT LOCKER
27	CHAIN AND ELM-TREE	40	WELL
	PUMPS	41	MAIN HOLD
28	MOORING BITTS	42	CABLE STORE
29	MANGER	43	MAIN MAGAZINE
30	ORLOP	44	FILLING ROOM

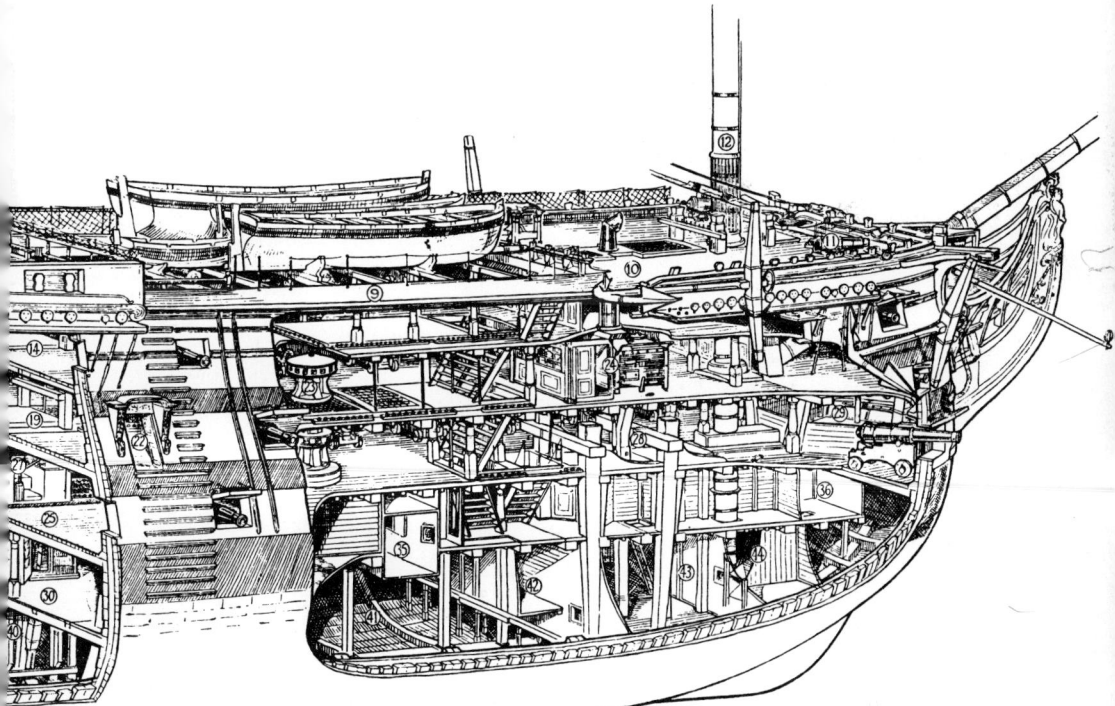

FOR FURTHER READING

CORBETT, SIR JULIAN STAFFORD. *The Campaign of Trafalgar*. New York: Longmans, 1910.

FORESTER, C. S. *Lord Nelson*. Indianapolis: Bobbs-Merrill, 1929.

GRENFELL, RUSSELL. *Nelson the Sailor* (2nd ed.). London: Faber, 1952.

JAMES, SIR WILLIAM MILBURNE. *Durable Monument: Horatio Nelson*. New York: Longmans, 1949.

MAINE, RENÉ. *Trafalgar: Napoleon's Naval Waterloo*. New York: Scribner, 1957.

POPE, DUDLEY. *Decision at Trafalgar*. Philadelphia: Lippincott, 1960.

SOUTHEY, ROBERT. *Life of Nelson*. New York: Dutton (Everyman Paperbacks), 1952.

WARNER, OLIVER. *Great Sea Battles* (chaps. 13, 14, 15). New York: Macmillan, 1963.

———. *Trafalgar*. New York: Macmillan, 1959.

———. *Victory: The Life of Lord Nelson*, Boston: Little, Brown (Atlantic Monthly Press), 1958.

——— and CHESTER W. NIMITZ. *Nelson and the Age of Fighting Sail*. New York: Harper (American Heritage), 1963.

INDEX